in case of emergency press

We are proud to acknowledge the Traditional Owners of country throughout Australia and to recognise their continuing connection to land, waters, and culture.
We pay our respects to their Elders.

We support recognition, reconciliation, and reparation.

God is a failure of imagination

in case of emergency press
https://icoe.com.au
Travancore, Victoria
Australia

Published by in case of emergency press 2024

Copyright © the author 2024

All rights reserved. Without limiting the rights under copyright reserved above, no part of this publication may be reproduced, stored in or introduced into a database and retrieval system or transmitted in any form or any means (electronic, mechanical, photocopying, recording or otherwise) without the prior written permission of both the owner of copyright and the above publishers.

ISBN: 978-1-7637749-1-9

God is a failure of imagination

Hello. I am the writer and you are the reader. I don't exist, and you do. You are holding this book in your hands. You are reading these words. I can speak to you, but you cannot speak to me. I may have once written these words, but they are now yours. You decide their meaning.

Everything you think about God is wrong.

If you have thought about God a great deal, you are probably an atheist.

If you have never thought about God, you are probably religious.

I (the non-existent) am neither, of course.

The reason that your idea of God is so hopelessly wrong is infinity. The nature of infinity precludes your ever being right. The nature of infinity precludes your ever approaching being right.

God is infinite.

You, the reader, are finite.

I, the writer, am not infinite, but I am beyond the finite world.

I am not real in the way that you, the reader, are real. You can touch. You can reason, think, change your mind, scratch you buttocks.

I do not exist. You can talk to yourself. You cannot talk to me.

God is infinite. You cannot talk to God. God is not of the finite world.

What else is infinite?

Nothing else is infinite.

It is ludicrous to think of infinity as being "single", but think of it this way: you cannot have two infinities. Two infinities would require that one infinity ended somewhere in order to distinguish it from another infinity.

Infinity does not end.

Let us think of something that we do not consider infinite: the number three.

You, who may or may not be a Christian, do not fear that I am interested in the peculiar idea of The Trinity. I am not discussing anything to do with any religion.

I am writing about God.

So, to return to the number three. Three is one of the very, very rare numbers which have a name. Most numbers do not. Most numbers have never been thought of, let alone been granted a name. Of course we can represent them mathematically, but three has a name. Like five or four or seven or a million. We have names for these few numbers. We compound these names to give names to other numbers, like "one million, two hundred and thirty four thousand, five hundred and sixty seven".

A clumsy name, perhaps, but still a name.

But most numbers are quite unnamed, because they are too big and there are too many of them. No one has ever thought of them. No one has ever had need of them.

I say "there are few numbers with names" because compared to the number of numbers without names (infinite), they are few.

That's the nature of infinity.

It isn't big. It is beyond big. Measurement has no meaning in the infinite world.

The writer again. Sorry to interrupt, but I do need to clarify that when I speak of "the infinite world", I use the word "world" to mean something like the mathematical idea of a set, the set of infinite things... although "things" implies a materiality which nothing infinite can have. Perhaps, the set of infinite concepts is better.

So, the number three. There is nothing infinite about it. It has no place in the infinite world. It is used in the world of "things" and it is quite useful there.

I have three apples. I see three butterflies. I will stand up in three minutes.

You got the idea long before I gave three examples.

Now, imagine the apparently infinite number of things in the universe. Imagine a mineral so rare that within the entire universe, there were only three examples of it.

You have done nothing but demonstrated that the number of things is not infinite. As soon as you can number any thing, infinity has vanished.

Within infinity, everything is infinite.

Three is of the finite world. As are you. As are your thoughts.

Think of God.

Your thoughts are of the finite world. Your thoughts are finite and constrained by finity.

God is infinite.

Your thoughts of God are hopelessly inadequate, worse than useless. Whatever you think or know or guess about God is nothing. What is three compared to the endlessness of numbers? As a proportion it is `1:infinity`.

Your concept of God is nothing, demonstrably nothing, for the same reason: `1:infinity`.

You cannot contemplate God.

Contemplate infinity: start at zero and count by 1. Tell me when you finish.

You cannot tell me. You cannot reach infinity, of course. You cannot reach me either, of course.

I am the writer. I can speak to you but you cannot speak to me.

God is a failure of imagination.

It cannot be otherwise.

www.ingramcontent.com/pod-product-compliance
Lightning Source LLC
Chambersburg PA
CBHW080326080526
44585CB00021B/2483